Allen Carr

No more fear of flying

ARCTURUS

ARCTURUS

This edition published in 2014 by Arcturus Publishing Limited
26/27 Bickels Yard, 151–153 Bermondsey Street,
London SE1 3HA, UK

ISBN: 978-1-78404-279-0
AD004268UK

Printed in the UK

To Sir Richard Branson with thanks for his amazing support for Allen Carr's Easyway method over more than 20 years

INTRODUCTION

Fear of flying is a debilitating condition that can have a devastating effect on your life. FOFs – people with fear of flying – put themselves through hell every time they take a flight, or else they avoid flying altogether, meaning they never get to enjoy the wonderful experiences that flying opens up: seeing the world, visiting friends and relations in farflung places, making the most of business opportunities.

Once upon a time seafarers feared that if they sailed too far west they would fall off the edge of the world. We now know that this fear had no foundation in reality, yet for those sailors it was very real and perfectly rational. Your fear of flying is every bit as real and understandable but, as this book will explain, it is no more founded in reality than the belief that the Earth is flat.

You will have heard that flying is the safest of all forms of transport, yet you're not convinced. The aim of this book is to convince you, not through the use of clever tricks or mind games, but by applying a method that has been proven to work time and time again.

The Allen Carr Easyway method has helped thousands of people to quit smoking, alcohol and other drugs, as well as to stop gambling, overeating and going into debt.

It works by unravelling the misconceptions that make people believe that they get some benefit from the very thing that's harming them.

This book applies the same method to unravel the misconceptions that make you believe flying is dangerous, despite all the evidence to the contrary. Unlike other methods, it does not require willpower.

All you have to do is read the book in its entirety, follow all the instructions and you cannot fail to cure your fear of flying.

Are you ready? Then let's go!

WHO NEEDS PLANES?

It's hard to believe that commercial flight has been around for less than a century – in the years since those first propeller planes carried passengers from London to Paris, it has grown out of all proportion. Today over 90,000 flights take off from around 9,000 airports around the world EVERY SINGLE DAY! At any given time there will be as many as 13,000 planes in the air over our planet.

Whether they're going on business, holiday or visiting friends and relations, millions of people rely on flying to get them where they want to go. And but for a minuscule exception, they all land safely at their destination.

LIFE WITHOUT FLYING

When you have a fear of flying you are left with two options:

1. Stay on the ground.
2. Grit your teeth and go through the nightmare that flying is for you.

If you choose option 1 you will either miss out on all the wonderful opportunities the world has to offer or waste days and weeks of your life taking slower modes of transport that eat into the time you could be spending enjoying your destination.

Choose option 2 and the chances are you'll be so wracked with apprehension that you'll ruin your entire trip.

THE METHOD THAT WORKS

With Allen Carr's Easyway, you will no longer have to settle for hell or the high road. This method will enable you to remove all your fears about flying and leave you champing at the bit to get on board and spread your wings.

The method makes it easy to conquer your fear of flying. All you have to do is follow a simple set of instructions. There are nine instructions in all.

THE MOST IMPORTANT INSTRUCTION

First instruction: follow all the instructions.

This might sound flippant but it's not. The method works like the combination of a safe. If I give you the combination and you follow it in order and in its entirety, the safe will open easily. But miss out any of the numbers, or use them in the wrong order, and the safe will remain firmly locked.

The first instruction is the most important. Follow this one and you cannot fail.

THE NEXT TWO INSTRUCTIONS

Second instruction: keep an open mind.

Question everything you think you know about flying.

Question everything I tell you in this book. Try not to make up your mind until you finish the book. The method relies on well-founded logic. You must give the logic room to breathe.

Third instruction: start off in a happy frame of mind.

I need you to trust me. Nothing bad is happening. You will not be asked to dig into your reserves of willpower or courage. All you have to do is follow the instructions. Think of all the marvellous gains you stand to make.

CURING THE BIGGEST FEAR IN THE WORLD

This method was originally devised to cure smoking, the world's number one addiction. It became a global phenomenon. It helped millions of smokers to quit easily and without willpower, by removing the misconceptions that surround nicotine addiction. By doing that, it removed the smokers' fear of stopping.

For you, there is no addiction but there is fear caused by misconceptions. This method will unravel those misconceptions and remove your fear.

HOW IS FLYING LIKE SMOKING?

In one sense fear of flying and nicotine addiction are complete opposites. Smoking is a pastime in which the one-in-two risk of death doesn't prevent smokers from participating; flying is a pastime in which people would love to participate but the less-than-one-in-several-million risk of death prevents them from doing so.

In other words… persuading someone to quit smoking is trying to convince them to stop doing something they think they enjoy, because it's dangerous.

Persuading someone to overcome their fear of flying is trying to convince them to do what they hate doing, because it isn't dangerous.

IN TWO MINDS

Ironically there are millions of people who suffer both. In fact, the more they think about flying, the more they want to smoke. They will tell you all the marvellous things that smoking does for them. Yet ask them if they'd encourage their children to smoke and they would give a unanimous 'NO!'

The problem is their brain is pulled in two directions: the rational part is telling them they shouldn't smoke, the irrational part is persuading them they need to carry on.

People with a fear of flying suffer a similar confusion: their rational brain is saying it's safe to fly, the irrational part is telling them it isn't.

MAKE THE RIGHT CHOICE

So you have a choice. Come down on the side of your rational mind or stick with the irrational. Smokers, despite their best efforts, usually end up sticking with their irrational desire to smoke. Do you want to go through the rest of your life missing out on all the marvellous pleasures that flying can bring, because you stuck with the irrational side of your brain?

WHY PEOPLE SMOKE

Despite all the studies into different types of smoker, there is only one reason why people smoke: they believe it gives them some kind of pleasure or crutch. They fear that quitting will make life unbearable.

They believe this because they have been fed a barrage of brainwashing since the day they were born.

The comparison I drew on page 15 is based on two pieces of false information.

The truth is:

1. Smoking is not a pastime, it's an addiction.
2. There is no enjoyment in smoking; smokers only think there is.

As soon as you understand this fact, quitting is easy.

REMOVE THE CONFUSION

Allen Carr's Easyway works by unravelling the brainwashing and replacing it with the truth. Once you can look beyond an illusion and see the truth, you change your mindset for ever.

Smokers remain smokers because they make the wrong choice. They choose the irrational over the rational. With this method, there is no choice to make. The irrational belief that smoking gives some kind of pleasure or crutch is removed and replaced with the knowledge that smoking gives no pleasure and actually increases the sense of insecurity.

By removing the irrational mindset that makes you afraid of flying, you can simply enjoy all the positive benefits of flying.

FEAR WITHOUT BASIS

Just like smoking, fear of flying is based on false beliefs.

Smokers fear that without smoking they won't be able to relax, concentrate, handle stress, enjoy social occasions, enjoy a meal and a drink, etc.

FOFs fear engine failure, mechanical failure, human error, acts of God, acts of terror, even that the laws of nature are against them.

These are all rational fears in their own right, but just as the smoker's fears are misplaced in terms of quitting smoking, your fears have no relevance when it comes to flying.

REMOVING THE SYMPTOMS, NEGLECTING THE CAUSE

If you had toothache, the dentist might give you a painkiller to ease the agony, but if he then did nothing about removing the cause of the pain, you'd be back day after day with the same complaint.

Other methods take the same approach to fear of flying. They try to help you overcome your fear so you can get through the journey, but all they are doing is treating the symptoms and not the cause.

This method doesn't help you overcome your fears, it removes them altogether.

I KNOW FLYING IS SAFE BUT I STILL FEAR IT

This is a phrase you'll often hear from FOFs. It shows the confusion I mentioned earlier. If you KNOW something is safe, you DON'T fear it.

The fact is you've been told that flying is safe by some very reputable people and you have no cause to doubt them… and yet you are not convinced. You still harbour fears that flying is NOT safe.

We need to remove those fears altogether.

YOU ARE NOT ALONE

Fear of flying can be a very lonely condition. Society tends to make fun of any show of fear, with the result that we keep our fears to ourselves. Or worse still, we don't listen to our fears and put ourselves through nightmarish and often dangerous situations, just to save face.

There is nothing abnormal or even unusual about fear of flying. In fact, anyone who claims not to have suffered it at least once in their life is either a fool or a liar.

FEAR IS A LIFESAVER

As the most powerful creature on the planet, the human being is equipped with a number of guiding forces that help to ensure his or her survival. One of those forces is fear. Fear protects us from danger. Without it, we would not see the danger in heights, water, fire, predators or whatever.

Fear is the cue for our 'fight or flight' instinct. It triggers a rush of hormones like adrenaline, which makes us momentarily and immediately stronger, faster, more alert. Without fear we would be sitting ducks.

BUT I FEEL LIKE A COWARD

Courage is not the same as fearlessness. Courage is acting in spite of your fear. If you see no danger in a situation, you don't need courage to get you through it.

This is the aim of this book: to change your mindset so that you see no danger in flying and therefore have no need to apply a single iota of courage.

That doesn't mean I'm going to blind you to the dangers in flying; it means I'm going to help you realize that the dangers are so minuscule as to be of no consideration.

THE GORILLA AND THE MIRROR

A gorilla in a zoo sees his reflection in a mirror for the first time and thinks it's a rival. He reacts with fear and aggression, just as he would if it were a real rival.

Very soon he comes to realize what the mirror is, a reflection of himself, and his behaviour changes. He no longer regards what he sees in the mirror as a danger, so his fear is not triggered.

Once you know and believe that there is no danger in flying, your fear will disappear.

PUT A NAME TO YOUR FEARS

Fear of flying comes in various forms:-

Fear of disaster – a lack of faith in the plane's ability to remain airborne

Claustrophobia – the fear of enclosed spaces

No control – a lack of faith in the people responsible for keeping the plane airborne

Vertigo – the fear of heights

Fear of fire – how does the fire brigade reach you at 35,000 feet?

Acts of God – the fear of bad weather, volcanic eruptions, etc.

All these fears can be grouped under one heading:

Fear of death

WHY WE THINK FLYING IS DANGEROUS

You've no doubt heard the old cliché that flying is statistically the safest of all forms of transport. So why does anyone perceive it to be dangerous?

On the very rare occasions when things do go wrong in the air, the results are dramatic. And there are two very powerful bodies that thrive on drama: the media and Hollywood.

Between them, they have concocted an image of flying as one big drama from take-off to landing. The media embellish their stories with sensational headlines and hysterical descriptions; Hollywood MAKES UP dramas about disasters in flight.

Thus the seeds of fear are sown.

DID YOU HEAR THE ONE ABOUT...?

There are countless jokes about flying – and each one involves something going wrong. We like to laugh in the face of disaster, so we invent disasters to give us an opportunity to laugh.

This might seem like a minor factor, but it all contributes to the general misconception that flying is fraught with danger.

FIRST-HAND ACCOUNTS

Ah, but what about those witnesses who tell horrific tales about their experience during a mid-air crisis? Panic! Terror! Chaos!

Ask yourself three questions:-

1. Who is relaying these accounts to the wider public?
2. What do the witnesses think is expected of them?
3. How come they're able to tell their tales at all?

The answer to question 1 is the media, and remember the media love a drama. For question 2, if you've ever been interviewed by a news reporter you'll know how they lead you on with their questions. And answer 3 is self-evident: whatever crisis they may have been through, they survived!

THE OBJECT OF THIS BOOK ISN'T TO MAKE YOU BRAVE

The object of this book is to remove your fear altogether, not to overcome it.

It is not cowardly to respond to fear by shying away from danger. That's exactly what we are designed by nature to do. Your fears are natural and real. It's the 'facts' underlying those fears that are not.

You have been fed those 'facts' by the media, Hollywood, jokes, other flyers and no doubt various other influences. But the indisputable truth is that flying is so safe that, once you understand and believe the true facts, it will be as irrational for you to fear flying as it is for the gorilla to fear his reflection in the mirror.

THE LIMITATIONS

The facts to which I refer in this book relate to flights that fall within what I call 'The Limitations'; that is, normal business, pleasure or holiday jet flights, including charter flights, departing from Western Europe, North America or Australasia. It includes return flights from anywhere in the world provided the return flight is with the same airline as the outward flight.

It doesn't include helicopter flights, balloon flights, airships, military aircraft, single-engined planes, privately owned planes or any form of glider.

In other words, I'm referring to the sort of flights most people take during their normal everyday lives.

DISPEL ALL NEGATIVE THOUGHTS

If you've recognised yourself among the fears I mentioned on page 27, you may have taken this as proof that you are weak or cowardly or lacking in some way that 'normal' people aren't.

Put that thought out of your mind!

As long as you believe flying to be dangerous, your fears are perfectly rational and normal. It is not a fault in you, but in the brainwashing you've been subjected to.

Remember the third instruction: start off in a happy frame of mind.

IS THIS AN EXERCISE IN POSITIVE THINKING?

No.

Positive thinking can't conquer a rational fear. The only way to do that is to unravel the misconceptions that make that fear seem rational. You can't do that if you are wracked with self-doubt and negativity. I need you to open your mind and see the facts as they really are. This is where the positive mindset comes in.

THE FOURTH INSTRUCTION

Fourth instruction: think positively!

Remember you have absolutely nothing to lose. If this method doesn't work for you, you will be no worse off than when you started.

If it does – and it can't fail if you follow all the instructions – you will gain something marvellous.

IF WE WERE MEANT TO FLY
WE'D BE BORN WITH WINGS

Perhaps you believe that flying goes against the laws of nature. But surely that rules out most other forms of transport. The wheel is not a product of nature, it is man-made. We are not designed by nature to zoom along rails at over 100mph but we've devised ways of doing so.

Being unnatural does not make something unsafe. Indeed, most medicines are unnatural. Do you regard modern medicine as unsafe?

BUT FLYING IS DIFFERENT

Agreed, none of those other unnatural things
I've mentioned involve leaving the ground.
And our basic understanding of gravity tells
us that the bigger and heavier an object is,
the harder it is for it to get off the ground and
the bigger the dent it makes when it falls.

A jet airliner is very big and very heavy.
And yet it does get off the ground – you've
seen it with your own eyes. So there must
be something else going on. Let's try to
understand what that is.

THE TRUTH ABOUT FLIGHT 1

The truth is that an aircraft, like a sailing boat, is in perfect harmony with the laws of nature.

If you follow motor racing you will know that one of the challenges facing racing car designers is how to keep it on the ground. Any object travelling at high speed has a natural tendency to take off. This is due to the effect of the wind rushing beneath it. Think of a hat or an umbrella on a windy day.

THE TRUTH ABOUT FLIGHT 2

An aircraft is designed to make the most of this natural phenomenon. Its wings are designed so that the wind rushing beneath them will cause an immense lifting force, and where the wings go, so the rest of the plane goes.

As with the racing car, the bigger question is how do you bring the plane back down to earth?

WHAT IF THE WIND DROPS?

A hat or an umbrella is susceptible to changes in the wind. A jet plane is not. Why? Because it creates its own wind.

Wind speed is relative to the speed at which you move. You will have noticed how, on a windy day, walking into the wind is difficult, but as soon as you turn your back and walk with the wind, it's as if there is no wind at all.

The huge engines on a plane thrust it forwards at such a speed that it will outrun any wind and thus the air will continue to flow backwards beneath its wings.

CONTROLLING THE WIND

Not only does a plane create its own wind, it also has complete control over the speed of that wind. By adjusting the thrust from the engines, the pilot can increase or decrease wind speed as he desires, to gain or lose height.

In other words, he is harnessing nature.

CONTROLLING THE SHAPE

As well as controlling the speed of the wind beneath the plane's wings, the pilot can also control the shape of the wings. By raising or lowering the flaps he can determine whether the wind causes the wings to lift or pushes them down.

At the same time, the plane is designed to fly through the air with the stability of an arrow. Just as the feather flight keeps an arrow stable in the air, the tail keeps a plane stable in flight. It is highly aerodynamic.

FOR THE PROOF, LOOK UP!

This may all sound very good in theory, but what about in practice?

If you need proof, look to the skies. At any given moment there are an estimated 30,000 aircraft flying perfectly safely and under complete control.

Since those early days of mechanical flight barely a century ago, aircraft designers have become highly adept at harnessing the power of nature and controlling it in fine detail.

TAKE-OFF AND LANDING

Asked what is the most dangerous stage of any flight, most people will guess at the take-off and landing. The question is misleading: no stage of any flight within The Limitations is dangerous.

However, because the few accidents that do occur often happen during take-off or landing, our brains are fooled into believing that these manoeuvres are actually dangerous.

A HUGE SAFETY MARGIN

For every flight a calculation is made of the exact speed the plane needs to reach before it will take off. This is based on the weight of the plane, its passengers, cargo and fuel.

The pilot will not attempt to take off until the plane has exceeded this speed by about 30 per cent.

If he takes off at 150mph, it means he could have taken off at 115mph. The safety margin removes any risk of the plane not taking off when the pilot commands it to do so.

WHAT ABOUT THE NATURAL LIFT?

If the plane is travelling more than fast enough to take off, how does the pilot keep it on the ground?

Like the spoilers on a racing car, the plane's wings are fitted with flaps that direct the wind in such a way that it creates a down force. As soon as he's ready to take off, the pilot reverses the position of the flaps and the plane lifts off the ground.

WHAT IF THE ENGINE FAILS?

If a plane relies on lift from the wind beneath its wings and that wind is created by the thrust from the engines, surely an engine failure would cause the plane to plummet?

Not so.

First, let's look at the likelihood of an engine failure. The average rate of failure of a modern jet engine within The Limitations is less than once in 10 million miles. Most pilots never experience a single engine failure in their entire career.

THE BACK-UP

On the rare occasions when engine failure does occur, a plane within The Limitations has a significant advantage over your car: a second engine – or in some cases a third and fourth. In all cases, just one engine is sufficient to keep the plane flying.

If all cars had a second engine, do you think we'd ever see poor motorists stranded at the side of the motorway?

The chances of a plane losing two engines at the same time are one in more than a hundred trillion.

THE ARROW EFFECT

When you fire an arrow through the air it travels in an arc. It doesn't reach a certain point and then plummet vertically to the ground.

The same is true of a plane. Even if you were to cut all the thrust from the engines, its impetus would keep it moving forward. At the same time its wings would continue to provide some lift. In other words, it would glide.

Modern jets are designed to glide. They don't drop vertically out of the air.

RUNWAY ROOM

If the pilot were to detect a fault during take-off, would he have room to abort before running out of runway?

YES!

If you want proof, take a day out to your nearest commercial airport and go to the observation deck. See how little of the available runway the pilots use as they take off and land, time after time, in all weathers, without a hint of danger.

OTHER MECHANICAL FAULTS

As with the engines, any vital safety function of an aircraft is doubled, tripled and sometimes quadrupled. For example, the hydraulics, which control the undercarriage and flaps, are worked from three separate systems, each of which could do the job on its own.

Even if all three were to malfunction at the same time, there is an emergency system, which would allow the plane to land safely.

WHAT IF A WING FALLS OFF?

That would be a concern. The wings are vital to keeping an aircraft airborne and so, not surprisingly, the manufacturers go to extreme lengths to make sure they don't come off.

Like every other vital component, they are subjected to stress tests that by far exceed anything they will encounter in actual flight.

To worry about a wing falling off at 500mph is equivalent to worrying about your arm becoming detached in a 10mph wind. It just cannot happen.

THE DREADED TURBULENCE

Even confident fliers can be unnerved by
turbulence. It can range in intensity from
a slight vibration to feeling as though the
plane is falling out of the sky! You will be
instructed to fasten your seatbelt. The flight
crew may well take their seats. There is
an air of tension throughout the plane. It's
enough to make anybody fearful.

But when you understand what turbulence
is, the fear disappears. It's all about
recognizing that what you are feeling is not a
sign of danger.

SO WHAT IS TURBULENCE?

Turbulence occurs when external air currents collide and become erratic. It most commonly occurs when going into cloud after take-off or before landing, or around bad weather. It sometimes occurs when there's not a cloud in the sky. This is known as clear-air turbulence or CAT.

Uncomfortable though it can be, turbulence represents no threat to a modern jet plane. The only danger is banging your head inside the plane if it suddenly drops a few feet, which is why you are told to strap in. In the history of modern aviation, not one single accident has been caused by turbulence.

WHY TURBULENCE FRIGHTENS US

The reason so many people find turbulence unnerving is that it feels like danger. Every movement of the plane is exaggerated in your mind, so a tiny drop in altitude feels as if you're plummeting several hundred feet. Rather than the plane cutting an aerodynamic line through the air, it feels as if it's being shaken from side to side.

The sense of danger is what frightens us. When you know beyond doubt there is no danger from turbulence, it immediately ceases to be frightening.

WHAT ABOUT AIR POCKETS?

Ah yes, air pockets – those sporadic vacuums that remove all lift because there is no air to rush beneath the wings. Air pockets are a myth. Lightning creates a vacuum for a split second before air rushes in to fill it. This is what causes the sound of thunder. It is impossible for a vacuum to exist in the atmosphere for more than a fraction of a second.

The myth of air pockets is down to turbulence, causing the plane to drop. What feels like a drop of several feet will usually be no more than a matter of inches.

HUMAN ERROR

There is human error in all things. We all
have off days. It only takes one dodgy pilot
and all those safety measures could be
thrown into jeopardy, couldn't they?

What if the pilot's had a bad day, is having
trouble at home, didn't get much sleep last
night or, worse still, has a drink problem?
We've all seen the movies. Anything's
possible when there's a human involved.

Forget it!

Do you know what it takes to become a
pilot?

THE EASY WAY TO BECOME A PILOT

That's one book we will never write for the simple reason that there is no easy way to become a pilot. The selection and training process for this career is incredibly rigorous. It is a highly competitive application process and only the crème de la crème make it through.

Once qualified, pilots are governed by a watertight set of rules and regulations and backed up by a team of experts who plot each flight for them. So they are never controlling the flight alone anyway.

WHY DO PILOTS ALWAYS SOUND SO COOL?

Because they are!

I don't mean in a James Dean sense, I mean in the sense that they are not stressed. The rosters that govern when and for how long a pilot flies are carefully planned to ensure against fatigue and stress. They are put through physical and psychological checks on a regular basis – more regular than probably any other profession – and they are subject to strict regulations governing the use of alcohol and other drugs.

When pilots fly they are in tip-top condition. And, like engines, should one break down, there is always another equally competent one ready to take over.

CAN I TRUST THE GROUND CREW?

Yes you can!

It wouldn't make sense to put the pilots through all those stringent checks if they were relying for their instructions on a bunch of happy-go-lucky buffoons on the ground, now would it?

All modern airlines are governed by safety standards that leave no margin for error and the staff on the ground take as much pride in their professionalism as do the pilots.

In short, whenever you fly you could not be putting your life in more competent hands.

ONE MISTAKE IS ALL IT TAKES, ISN'T IT?

In a word, NO!

The airline business is not so much a belt and braces affair as two belts and several pairs of braces. The entire system is designed to cover for human error. If one mistake is made, there are so many layers of safety checks that it will be picked up before it gets anywhere near the flight itself.

Whenever a mistake is made, it is investigated and procedures put in place to make sure it never happens again.

AIR TRAFFIC CONTROL

Imagine a motorway on which all the cars travel at the same speed, in the same lane, with half a mile between them. Can you imagine there ever being any accidents?

This is how air traffic is controlled.

We only tend to hear about air traffic controllers when they go on strike. They deserve more recognition for what they do. Like the pilots and ground staff, they are highly trained, intelligent professionals backed up by an array of failsafes.

They don't make mistakes.

WHAT ABOUT ALL THESE NEAR MISSES WE HEAR ABOUT?

A near miss is simply the term used when two aircraft become closer than the stipulated distance laid down. Contrary to the wishes of the drama-hungry media, it does not mean their wing tips have nearly touched or they've practically rubbed noses in mid-air. Far from it. Incidences of mid-air collisions of flights within The Limitations are less than one in several billion. Such is the safety margin within which air traffic control operates throughout the world.

THE THREAT OF TERRORISM

There have been some horrific examples of hijacking and sabotage on flights in the years of modern commercial flight, as a result of which security on airlines is now far tighter than any other mode of transport.

Before 9/11, airport security screened 5 per cent of baggage. Today 100 per cent of baggage is screened. In addition, the technology for detecting explosives and other weapons has advanced considerably and the layers of security that any would-be terrorist would have to penetrate have multiplied several-fold.

SEE THROUGH THE FOG

If you suffer from fear of flying, it doesn't help when you hear there's a likelihood of fog in the region you're flying in.

Fog is a Hollywood favourite: we've all seen the image of the confused pilot, trying to find his way through dense fog, when suddenly a mountain looms into sight too late for him to avoid.

It makes for a good drama but it has nothing to do with modern flying within The Limitations.

AVOIDING FOG ALTOGETHER

There's a lot less fog at airports these days, thanks to anti-pollution legislation, but remember, flight regulations are designed to rule out any element of risk. If there is a danger of fog or other weather conditions posing a threat to the safety of the flight, the plane will not take off.

Before each flight a plan is prepared, which takes into account weather conditions throughout the entire flight. This is based on extremely accurate information. Where there is a threat of bad weather, a course will be plotted to avoid it.

PILOTS DON'T NEED TO SEE OUT

Unlike the hapless pilot in the movies, modern pilots don't see where they're going by peering through the windscreen. The technology that guides planes from A to B also enables pilots to take off and land even when visibility is zero.

The instruments in the cockpit tell the pilots their exact coordinates and altitude and they are so skilled at using them that they can guide the plane in to land as if they are playing a video game.

Fog is no cause for alarm whatsoever.

WHAT IF THE PLANE RUNS OUT OF FUEL?

This is where the concept of being in the air seems much more dangerous than driving a car. When a car runs out of fuel it may splutter a bit and then roll powerlessly into the side of the road. It's an inconvenience and you feel stupid, but in most instances it's not dangerous. Run out of fuel 35,000 feet up and it's a different story.

Of course it is! That's why careful calculations are made before each flight to make sure that the plane has more than enough fuel on board to complete the journey, and more to allow for contingencies.

WHAT IF THE FUEL TANK LEAKS?

The chances of a fuel tank springing a leak in mid-flight are minuscule. These components are checked far more stringently than you check the components on your car. When was the last time your car's fuel tank sprang a leak?

Flight crews monitor fuel consumption constantly, so in the unlikely event that a leak should occur, they will quickly spot the problem and divert if necessary to land safely at the nearest airport.

WHAT IF THE PLANE IS THOUSANDS OF MILES FROM LAND?

It won't be. Even flight paths that crisscross the major oceans will pass within reach of air bases like the one on Ascension Island in the middle of the Atlantic, which has been used for fuel stops in the past.

Most air routes, though they fly over the sea for reasons of noise and economy, will always be within a few hundred miles of land. I have failed to find one single incident of aircraft within The Limitations having to ditch in the sea.

DO YOU HAVE VERTIGO?

Only as far as the bus stop.

You can thank The Goons for that joke.
Vertigo, or fear of heights, is no joke for those
who suffer with it. Like all the fears we've
tackled so far, there is nothing irrational
about vertigo, although we should really
give it a different name: it's not so much fear
of heights as fear of falling off.

If the sense of being a long way off the
ground induces fear in you, it stands to
reason that flying should be about as
frightening as it gets.

But a lot of people who suffer with vertigo
feel no fear at all in a plane.

FEAR OF FALLING OFF

It's not the height itself that induces fear but the possibility of falling off and hitting the ground. In other words, the fear of death.

Height doesn't equal danger. Take Lake Titicaca for example.

If you stood on the shores of the lake you would have absolutely no sensation of vertigo. Yet you would be standing 12,500 feet above sea level.

Stand on a narrow ledge 125 feet up, however, and there would be something odd if you didn't feel frightened.

A MATTER OF TRUST

Vertigo boils down to trust: trust in the integrity of the structure you're standing on and trust in yourself.

To the vertigo sufferer, a balcony or a cable is not trustworthy. All it takes is for that railing to come away, or that cable to snap, or for you to lean over too far and down you'll plummet.

Of course, this is not really the case but if you have no trust in the structure supporting you, you will sense danger and fear will be the result. By the same token, if you feel completely safe you will have no fear of heights.

WHY SOME VERTIGO SUFFERERS HAVE NO FEAR OF FLYING

If there was any sense that you could fall out of a plane in mid-flight, you wouldn't have to be a confirmed vertigo sufferer to be afraid. Anyone in their right mind would be petrified that they might tip out and plummet thousands of feet to the ground.

But people don't fall out of planes. You are comfortably enclosed in a sealed cabin and wherever the plane goes, you will go too.

Once you understand and believe that you can trust a plane to stay airborne, that the forces of nature are keeping it there, you will no longer fear any danger of falling.

IF YOU KNEW IN ADVANCE THAT YOUR PLANE WOULD LAND SAFELY, WOULD YOU STILL FEAR THE FLIGHT?

A surprising number of people answer yes to this question.

Why?

Because they are not entirely convinced that what they know is true. And the reason for that is because they are not allowing themselves to see the facts. They are not opening their minds.

If this is you, remember the third and fourth instructions. Start off in a happy frame of mind and think positively. If you remain in a negative frame of mind you will continue to allow your misconceptions to override the facts.

PUT THE ODDS IN PERSPECTIVE

You know that the chances of something
bad happening to you when flying are
minuscule, yet you've convinced yourself
that if there is a one in a billion chance, you
will be that one in a billion.

If I asked you how you think you're going to
die, would you put 'plane crash' at the top of
your list? Would it even be on your list? No?
Then there's no logic in believing you are in
danger of death as soon as you set foot on a
plane!

THE FIFTH INSTRUCTION

How do you feel when you board a train?
Excited perhaps, if you're going somewhere
special. More often than not we board trains
without even thinking how we feel. We don't
torture ourselves with unnecessary thoughts
about the disasters that might befall this of
all trains.

Catching a plane is no different. In fact, it's
a lot safer. So here's the fifth instruction: go
for it!

Accept that you are going to take that first
or next flight whether you like it or not.
Now you have a choice: torture yourself
with negativity or fill your head with all the
positive facts and get on with it.

IN THE SWIM

Removing your fear of flying is easy
provided you follow all the instructions, but
don't underrate yourself.

There are many things in life we learn to do
and the learning process means removing
a certain amount of fear. Swimming, riding
a bicycle and passing your driving test are
all examples. We begin by feeling afraid
and apprehensive about our ability to
master them but when we do, the joy is
immeasurable.

You have this feeling to look forward to.

THE WHOLE POINT OF FLYING

To help you adopt a positive mindset, think of all the marvellous gains you will make by removing your fear of flying. You will be able to see the world, get to places faster, visit friends and relations you may have avoided seeing because of your fear, and simply enjoy the amazing sensation of flying through the air in total comfort.

The sixth instruction is what flying is all about: enjoy it!

You have so much to gain.

CLAUSTROPHOBIA

For some FOFs, it's the fear of being in an enclosed space that scares them away from flying.

An aircraft is undoubtedly an enclosed space but if the fear is specifically that – being in an enclosed space – why aren't the same people afraid of toilet cubicles or dressing rooms in shops?

In fact, most shops are smaller than the cabin of a passenger jet and yet you don't hear of claustrophobics avoiding the shops.

WHAT DOES THE ENCLOSED SPACE REPRESENT?

Think about other common locations that induce claustrophobia.

Lifts
Cable cars
Tunnels
Tube trains

All these examples have something more than just being an enclosed space. They are situations in which you might imagine other dangers, such as a snapped cable or a tunnel collapse. Isn't it the fear of being entombed that causes claustrophobia in a tunnel? Isn't it the fear of the lift or cable car plummeting to the ground that makes those things feel claustrophobic?

STOP THINKING ABOUT WHAT COULD GO WRONG!

The fear of being entombed or plummeting to your death is completely normal and rational. What is not rational is worrying yourself that such a thing could happen in the situations I've mentioned.

People who make lifts will have one overriding concern: the safety of everyone who ever travels in their lift. They will have considered the possibility of a cable snapping and built in failsafes to cover it. Like the multiple engines on a plane, lifts run on several cables, each of which is strong enough to support the lift on its own.

The danger you perceive does not exist.

UNDERSTANDING DISPELS FEAR

If you feel claustrophobic inside an aircraft, it's because you believe that you're putting yourself in danger. I've explained why the perceived dangers of flying are so minuscule as not to be worth worrying about. Once you understand and believe that flying is not dangerous, you will not feel claustrophobic inside a plane, any more than you would inside a comfortable restaurant.

Only if you think the plane is inherently dangerous will you feel a fear of being enclosed within it.

TAKE THE LIFT TEST

Here's a way to try out your new mindset before you go anywhere near a plane. Try it out in a lift.

Remind yourself that the lift is not supported by one cable but by six or maybe eight, each of which is strong enough to support the lift and a full complement of passengers.

Remember that the lift designers have built in every possible measure to ensure the safety of every single passenger who ever rides in that lift.

Now keep those positive thoughts in mind and enjoy riding that lift.

When you've removed your fear of lifts you'll know that you'll be able to remove your fear of flying.

FLYING THROUGH FEAR

Not all FOFs avoid flying altogether. Some brave souls push themselves to catch flights despite their fear. They put themselves through hell and ironically think their fear is a sign of cowardice. The opposite is true. Courage is surely acting in spite of fear.

There is another fear at play: the fear of social ridicule. Social pressure can drive us to do things we really don't want to do. FOFs often fear that society will ridicule them for being afraid. But until you believe flying is safe, your fear is perfectly normal and rational.

GOOD AND BAD DRIVERS

If you are being driven by a good driver, the road feels like a safe place. Even the bad drivers out there don't seem to be a threat because you trust your driver to be ready to avoid them.

If you're being driven by a bad driver, the road feels like a lethal place. Every other lunatic seems to be attracted to your car and it's impossible to relax and enjoy the journey.

It's all about trust. If you don't trust your driver, the same road conditions that felt safe with the good driver suddenly appear to be a threat.

WHEN THE PLANE DOOR CLOSES

It takes courage to ask someone to stop the car and let you out because you don't feel safe. It would take a lot more courage to ask to be let off a plane for the same reason. Once that cabin door closes you have a choice: allow all your fears to gang up on you and make the experience a nightmare; or keep in mind all the facts you have learnt about flying and the lengths they go to to ensure your safety, remove all sense of danger and make the flight enjoyable.

DANGER IS THE KEY

Once you realize that flying is absolutely safe, all the associated fears like claustrophobia, vertigo, panic attacks and lack of control disappear.

Remove that sense of danger and you remove the fear.

Then you can begin to see flying as it really is: an exhilarating, pleasurable experience that can take your life literally into new realms.

Hopefully by now you're starting to believe that there is no danger in flying worth worrying about. Much better to think about all the benefits it can bring you.

DON'T OBSESS
ABOUT THE DETAILS

While it's important to know and
understand certain aspects of commercial
flight in order to allay your fears that it is
dangerous, it can be counter-productive if
you pay too much attention to the details.

You've heard of 'backseat driver syndrome'?
It applies to car passengers who spend the
entire journey focusing on what the driver
is doing and trying to pre-empt every
brake, steer and gear change with their own
imaginary controls. It's a nightmare for the
passenger and everyone around them. Far
better to relax, switch off and let the driver
get on with it.

The same applies on a plane. You have the
best pilots money can buy. Leave it to them,
relax and enjoy the journey.

FOCUS ON YOUR GOAL

When an athlete embarks on the years of training required to become an Olympic medallist, he or she will acquire the motivation to take on the hard work required by visualizing their goal. That moment when they stand on the podium, medal round their neck, the culmination of all they have worked for – that is their ultimate focus.

For you, it's not your first or next flight that is most important but the achievement of your goal: to remove your fear of flying.

YOUR BIG ADVANTAGE

In fact, you have two advantages over the athlete. The first is that your challenge is nowhere near as arduous. All you have to do is follow all the instructions and you can not only enjoy the achievement but the preparation too.

Your biggest advantage is that the athlete has to compete against hundreds or even thousands of others all pursuing the same goal. Only one can succeed. But there is no limit to the number of people who can enjoy flying. You don't have to beat anybody!

REMEMBER THE INSTRUCTIONS

1. Follow all the instructions
2. Keep an open mind
3. Start off in a happy frame of mind
4. Think positively
5. Go for it
6. Enjoy it

YOUR JOURNEY STARTS HERE

What do you think is the most important moment for the Olympic athlete? When they stand upon the podium watching their national flag being raised? When they run their first qualifying race? When they first set foot on the training track?

No. It's the moment they first decide to go for it. Without that moment, nothing else happens.

The preparation for your next flight doesn't start when you arrive at the airport. It has already started and the important time is

NOW!

BEFORE YOU REACH THE PLANE

If you need any further proof that fear of flying is a state of mind and has no basis in reality, consider the fact that most FOFs experience the fear before they get anywhere near a plane. It's not the plane itself that frightens them, it's the thought of the plane.

If you allow yourself to be obsessed with negative thoughts you will torture yourself imagining all the things that could possibly go wrong.

Instead, spend your time thinking of all the positive reasons for flying and reaffirming all you have learnt about how safe it is.

DON'T THINK OF ELEPHANTS

You are going to catch a flight – that is a fact. Don't try to pretend it's not happening. The seventh instruction is:

don't try to take your mind off flying

Trying to put it out of your mind may sound like a way to get through the time between now and your flight but all you will do is create a phobia. If I told you not to think of elephants, what's the first thing that comes into your mind?

Exactly!

Allow yourself to think about your flight, think positive thoughts and focus on the enjoyment you are going to get from removing your fear.

YOU HAVE A CHOICE

If you think I'm making it sound simple to change your mindset, that's because it is. You have a choice. You can allow yourself to go on torturing yourself with negative thoughts about all the imaginary things that could go wrong, or you can focus on all the facts I've told you and enjoy the anticipation of achieving your goal. It really is a matter of choice.

By all means go back and remind yourself of any facts that you're still in doubt about and keep following the instructions.

LET THE HOLIDAY MAKE THE FLIGHT

Remember why you are catching your flight. Where is it taking you? What will you do when you get there?

Spend your time worrying about the flight and you will not only have an unpleasant flight, you will ruin your entire trip.

On the other hand, the anticipation of a great trip can add to the enjoyment of the flight.

See the flight as a means to an end – all part of something marvellous that is happening.

HOW WILL YOU KNOW YOU'VE LOST YOUR FEAR OF FLYING?

Many people who suffer fear of flying never get on a plane in their entire lives. How can they possibly know, you might argue, that they are afraid of flying if they never actually fly?

The fact is they are not afraid of flying itself but the idea of flying. Thanks to the brainwashing, they don't need to experience flight to be convinced that it's dangerous.

Fear of flying doesn't come from being in the situation but from anticipating it.

WHEN YOU KNOW, YOU KNOW

The process can be reversed just as easily. Remove the misconceptions and you can be absolutely convinced that you no longer have a fear of flying long before you get to the airport.

The same applies to smokers. Before they quit, smokers wonder how they will know when they are free of their nicotine addiction. The fact is you know as soon as you succeed in unravelling the brainwashing and seeing the truth. With Allen Carr's Easyway, you know you've quit smoking before you stub out your final cigarette.

SOMETHING TO LOOK FORWARD TO

Let's go back to the Olympic medallist and the visualization of the end goal. What I want you to think about isn't:

'Won't it be lovely if I can find the courage to fly so that I can enjoy a holiday with my family and friends or accompany my partner on a business trip?'

But

'The holiday or business trip isn't important. The important thing is that I'm going to shed the shackles of fear of flying. I'm going to escape from this prison.'

Your exhilaration will be in achieving that goal.

PREPARE YOUR MIND

Between now and the flight, keep a happy and positive frame of mind. Don't worry that you keep thinking about it. It's what you are thinking that is important. Remember you have the choice.

Your eighth instruction is this: from now on you are going to take control

Flying is incredibly safe – fact. So if you find yourself thinking about it, enjoy doing so.

LET THE BUTTERFLIES FLY

If, between now and the flight, you experience butterflies in your stomach, don't worry. Butterflies are a sign that something marvellous is about to happen. Think of a footballer about to walk out for a cup final. The jitters they feel are accompanied by a feeling of exhilaration.

Unlike the footballer, however, you cannot lose. Provided you follow all the instructions, you have no rival force facing you that can prevent you from winning.

WHEN THE MOMENT ARRIVES

The day of the flight can be stressful for many reasons. The plane won't wait for you if you're late. You won't be allowed through customs if your passport is not up to date. There are many arrangements to take care of but you can avoid all the stress by planning well in advance.

Make a list of all the essentials:-

Tickets
Passport
Money
Insurance
Baggage allowance
Check-in time

The more you prepare in advance, the more enjoyable the day of the flight will be.

ARRIVE EARLY

I strongly recommend that you plan to arrive at the airport at least an hour before your check-in time. Late taxis, traffic jams, wrong directions… there are plenty of things that can hold you up so allow time for all eventualities. The aim is to avoid any unnecessary stress.

If it all goes smoothly and you find yourself with an hour to kill at the airport, that's wonderful. Enjoy the experience. Have a cup of tea. Read a book. Relax.

CHOOSING YOUR SEATS

Forget anything you may have heard about whether it's statistically safest to sit at the front or tail end. It's irrelevant. It's not dangerous wherever you choose to sit.

The only seating considerations concern how you want to enjoy your flight. Do you want to be by a window, so you can look at the wonderful views? Or would you prefer an aisle seat, so you can chat to your friends and stretch your legs when you feel like it?

THE PAPERWORK

Avoid stress when checking in your luggage by having all your necessary documents – passport and ticket or boarding pass – ready and easily accessible. Keep them together to avoid any last-minute rummaging through suitcases, panicking that you might have left them at home.

Keep them handy for the next stage, passport control. Keep your documents easily accessible because you will need them again at the boarding gate. But put them somewhere secure, like an inside pocket.

SECURITY SCANNING

If you want an idea of how secure flying has become, this is the place. By this stage you will be carrying hand luggage only. Make sure there are no liquids in it of more than 100ml in volume. If there are, these may be removed and confiscated.

Next you will be required to remove all metal objects, including belts, and often your shoes as well. While all these objects are passing through the scanner, you will pass through a scanner too, while being scrutinized by at least two security officers.

There's no need to feel intimidated. The whole process is reassuringly rigorous.

THE DEPARTURE LOUNGE

If you've arrived in plenty of time as advised, you can spend some time enjoying the shops, bars and restaurants of the departure lounge. Of course, this place is designed to relieve excited travellers of their hard-earned cash by selling them things they simply can't resist at the last minute. It's all duty-free and you'll be required to show your boarding pass when paying.

Don't worry about losing track of your flight. There are plenty of screens showing flight information, and listen out for announcements. It helps to find out early on which gate you're boarding from and where that gate is, especially in the larger airports.

DELAYS

Delays are a common cause of stress, whether you suffer from fear of flying or not. Because travellers are keen to get to their destination, a delay can become a cause for intense scrutiny.

A crowd gathers round the information desk, staff make themselves absent, tempers become frayed, voices are raised, insults are thrown about.

It's important that you avoid this sort of stress if you are to remain positive about your flight. Delays are an inevitable consequence of a highly safety-conscious industry. Don't interpret them as a sign of potential danger, but as evidence of experts taking extra care to ensure that there is no danger.

ENJOY THE DOWNTIME

There is nothing you can do about flight delays, so the best thing you can do is take them in your stride and make sure you have something enjoyable to do to kill time, such as reading a good book. At most airports there will be shops and restaurants where you can enjoy the rare experience of having time on your hands.

Remember, whatever the reason for the delay, it is bound to be in the interests of safety.

RELAXANTS

For some fliers, this is the time when they turn to so-called relaxants like alcohol or Valium to help them get through the ordeal. This is a case of tackling the symptoms, not the cause.

In fact, these so-called relaxants don't even remove the symptoms of fear of flying, they just obliterate them from your mind. And when they wear off the symptoms feel worse.

Once you've removed the fear, you won't need alcohol, Valium or any other crutch.

THE BOARDING GATE

Allow yourself plenty of time to get from the departure lounge to the boarding gate. It can sometimes be a long walk and if you've ever seen someone running for a plane, you'll know how stressful that can be!

At the gate you can sit and wait for the cue to begin boarding. Make sure you've still got your passport and boarding pass handy, then relax. You will see people beginning to queue in impatient anticipation before they are called. Resist the temptation to join them. You're all catching the same plane and there's room for everyone.

BOARDING

If you want to avoid the scramble for seats, you can discreetly inform the staff when you arrive at the boarding gate that you are a nervous flier and ask to be allowed on first. They will go out of their way to accommodate you.

Alternatively, wait until the queue has died down and board near the end, at your own pace. Unless you particularly want to enjoy the view or you'd like to be by the aisle, it doesn't matter where you end up sitting, or where your luggage gets stowed.

ONCE THE DOORS
ARE CLOSED

When the cabin crew are satisfied that every
passenger who should be on the flight has
boarded, they will close the aircraft doors.
You will be asked to fasten your seatbelt,
fold your seat tray up, put your seat in the
upright position and have your armrest
down.

As the plane taxis slowly towards the start
of the runway, the crew will demonstrate
the safety procedure. You are advised to pay
attention, but don't give it too much thought.
The chances of ever having to follow the
procedure are minuscule.

TAKE-OFF

Taking off in an aeroplane is an exhilarating experience. It is the safest way you will ever experience acceleration from 0 to 150mph in a matter of seconds.

You know now that when the plane reaches a certain speed, the forces of nature will cause it to take off. Unless you're looking out of the window, you probably won't even notice when it does.

The first major change you'll notice is when the pilot executes a turn. Like a bicycle, a plane turns by leaning the way it wants to go. Don't be alarmed by this. It's perfectly natural.

BUMPS, SQUEAKS, PINGS AND ROARS

All that's left now is for the pilot to raise the undercarriage. You've seen how big those wheels are – it takes a powerful hydraulic system to raise and lower those things. Not surprisingly, it makes a bit of noise.

Flying is a remarkably peaceful experience, but every so often you will hear a noise that might alarm you. The ping of the intercom, the roar of the engines as the pilot demands more thrust. These are all perfectly normal aspects of every single flight.

DON'T TRY TO FLY THE PLANE!

Resist the temptation to react to every bump, squeak, ping and roar by trying to analyse what's going on. You will only torture yourself for no logical reason.

The pilots are responsible for assessing the performance of the plane. They are extremely well qualified to do so, whereas you are not. So leave it to them, trust in their expertise, accept that every noise you hear is a normal, everyday aspect of flying and relax and enjoy the experience.

This is your ninth and last instruction:

don't try to fly the plane!

ENJOY THE FLIGHT

Whatever form of transport you take,
whether or not you enjoy the journey
depends on whether or not you feel safe.
If you feel in danger you will not enjoy the
journey.

As the plane levels off, remind yourself
of this: you are now in one of the safest
environments you've been in during the
last 24 hours. You've crossed roads, you've
survived the car, taxi or train ride to the
airport, you've been up and down escalators
and staircases. As you sit back in your
padded seat on board the flight, you are now
statistically safer than you were in any of
those situations.

GIVE YOUR FEAR THE DAY OFF

Fear is a friend – it protects us from danger.

Fear of flying is perfectly rational – but it is based on misconceptions.

Remove the misconceptions – remove the fear.

There is no rational reason for holding on to a fear when you know there is no danger. If you still harbour one or more of the many fears associated with fear of flying, you have not followed all the instructions. You have not opened your mind and allowed yourself to see the truth:

FLYING IS NOT DANGEROUS.

It is time to let go of your fear.

I CAN'T WAIT TO SEE IF IT'S WORKED!

You don't have to wait for anything.

As soon as you know you have the solution to a problem, the problem is already solved. Once you believe flying is not dangerous, your fear will be cured.

Fear of flying is purely mental. All you have to do is change what's in your mind from misconceptions to facts. When you achieve that, you don't have to go through the next flight and land safely to know that your fear has gone. You will know before you even set foot aboard the plane.

CLEAR FOR TAKE-OFF

The beautiful truth is that flying is incredibly safe. If you have followed all the instructions and opened your mind, you should now look forward to your next flight with a feeling of excitement and elation. Just like the explorers who discovered that the Earth is round, you are free of the fears that have held you back.

The world is your oyster.

Where you choose to go is entirely up to you. Happy travels.

THE INSTRUCTIONS

1. Follow all the instructions

2. Keep an open mind

3. Start off in a happy frame of mind

4. Think positively

5. Go for it

6. Enjoy it

7. Don't try to take your mind off flying.

8. You are going to take control

9. Don't try to fly the plane

TELL ALLEN CARR'S EASYWAY
ORGANISATION THAT YOU'VE ESCAPED
Leave a comment on www.allencarr.com, email
yippee@allencarr.com, like our Facebook page
www.facebook.com/AllenCarr
or write to the Worldwide Head Office address
shown below.

ALLEN CARR'S EASYWAY CLINICS
The following list indicates the countries where
Allen Carr's Easyway To Stop Smoking Clinics
are currently operational. Check www.
allencarr.com for latest additions to this list.
The success rate at the clinics, based on the
three month money-back guarantee, is over 90
per cent.

Selected clinics also offer sessions that deal
with alcohol, other drugs, and weight issues.
Please check with your nearest clinic, listed
below, for details.

Allen Carr's Easyway guarantees that you will
find it easy to stop at the clinics or your money
back.

ALLEN CARR'S EASYWAY
Worldwide Head Office
Park House, 14 Pepys Road, Raynes Park,
London SW20 8NH ENGLAND
Tel: +44 (0)208 9447761
Email: mail@allencarr.com
Website: www.allencarr.com

Worldwide Press Office
Tel: +44 (0)7970 88 44 52
Email: jd@allencarr.com

UK Clinic Information and Central Booking
Line 0800 389 2115 (Freephone)

UNITED KINGDOM	JAPAN
REPUBLIC OF IRELAND	LATVIA
AUSTRALIA	LEBANON
AUSTRIA	LITHUANIA
BELGIUM	MAURITIUS
BRAZIL	MEXICO
BULGARIA	NETHERLANDS
CANADA	NEW ZEALAND
CHILE	NORWAY
COLOMBIA	PERU
CYPRUS	POLAND
DENMARK	PORTUGAL
ECUADOR	ROMANIA
ESTONIA	RUSSIA
FINLAND	SERBIA
FRANCE	SINGAPORE
GERMANY	SLOVENIA
GREECE	SOUTH AFRICA
GUATEMALA	SOUTH KOREA
HONG KONG	SPAIN
HUNGARY	SWEDEN
ICELAND	SWITZERLAND
INDIA	TURKEY
ISRAEL	UKRAINE
ITALY	USA

Visit www.allencarr.com to access your
nearest clinic's contact details.

OTHER ALLEN CARR PUBLICATIONS

Allen Carr's revolutionary Easyway method is available in a wide variety of formats, including digitally as audiobooks and ebooks, and has been successfully applied to a broad range of subjects.

For more information about Easyway publications, please visit
www.easywaypublishing.com

Stop Smoking Now (with hypnotherapy CD)
ISBN: 978-1-84837-373-0

Stop Smoking with Allen Carr (with 70-minute audio CD)
ISBN: 978-1-84858-997-1

The Illustrated Easy Way to Stop Smoking
ISBN: 978-1-84837-930-5

Finally Free!
ISBN: 978-1-84858-979-7

The Easy Way for Women to Stop Smoking
ISBN: 978-1-84837-464-5

The Illustrated Easy Way for Women to Stop Smoking
ISBN: 978-1-78212-495-5

How to Be a Happy Non-Smoker
ISBN: 978-0-572-03163-3

Smoking Sucks (Parent Guide with 16 page pull-out comic)
ISBN: 978-0-572-03320-0

No More Ashtrays
ISBN: 978-1-84858-083-1

The Little Book of Quitting
ISBN: 978-1-45490-242-3

The Only Way to Stop Smoking Permanently
ISBN: 978-0-14-024475-1

The Easy Way to Stop Smoking
ISBN: 978-0-71819-455-0

How to Stop Your Child Smoking
ISBN: 978-0-14027-836-1

The Easy Way to Control Alcohol
ISBN: 978-1-84837-465-2

No More Hangovers
ISBN: 978-1-84837-555-0

Lose Weight Now (with hypnotherapy CD)
ISBN: 978-1-84837-720-2

No More Diets
ISBN: 978-1-84837-554-3

The Easy Weigh to Lose Weight
ISBN: 978-0-14026-358-9

The Easy Way to Stop Gambling
ISBN: 978-1-78212-448-1

No More Gambling
Ebook

No More Worrying
ISBN: 978-1-84837-826-1

Allen Carr's Get Out of Debt Now
ISBN: 978-1-84837-98-7

No More Debt
Ebook

The Easy Way to Enjoy Flying
ISBN: 978-0-71819-458-3

Burning Ambition
ISBN: 978-0-14103-030-2

Packing It In The Easy Way (the autobiography)
ISBN: 978-0-14101-517-0

DISCOUNT VOUCHER FOR
ALLEN CARR'S EASYWAY CLINICS

Recover the price of this book when
you attend an
Allen Carr's Easyway Clinic
anywhere in the world.

Allen Carr has a global network
of clinics where he guarantees
you will find it easy to stop
smoking or your money back.

The success rate based on this
money-back guarantee is over 90 per cent.

When you book your appointment
mention this voucher and you will
receive a discount to the value
of this book. Contact your
nearest clinic for more information
on how the sessions work and
to book your appointment.
Not valid in conjunction with any other offer.